# PORTUGUESE SLANGUAGE

A *FUN* VISUAL GUIDE TO PORTUGUESE TERMS AND PHRASES BY MIKE ELLIS

GIBBS SMITH

First Edition
19 18 17 16 15 5 4 3 2 1



Published by
Gibbs Smith
P.O. Box 667
Layton, Utah 84041

1.800.835.4993 orders
www.gibbs-smith.com

Designed by michelvrana.com

Gibbs Smith books are printed on paper produced from sustainable PEFC-certified forest/controlled wood source. Learn more at www.pefc.org.
Printed and bound in Hong Kong

Library of Congress Cataloging-in-Publication Data

Ellis, Mike, 1961–
Portuguese slanguage : a fun visual guide to Portuguese terms and phrases / Mike Ellis.
— First Edition.
pages cm
ISBN 978-1-4236-3934-3
1. Portuguese language—Conversation and phrase books—English. I. Title.
PC5073.E55 2015
469'.83421—dc23

2014037258

# CONTENTS

# HOW TO USE THIS BOOK

If you have always wanted to learn the basics of Portuguese, but traditional methods seemed overwhelming or intimidating, this book is for you! Just follow the directions below and soon you'll be able to say dozens of words and phrases in Portuguese.

• Follow the illustrated prompts and say the phrase quickly and smoothly. Emphasize the words or syllables highlighted in red. A strikethrough means don't pronounce that letter.

• Learn to string together words or phrases to create many more phrases.

• The words and phrases are sorted alphabetically within each chapter to make finding them easier.

• Draw your own pictures to help with memorization and pronunciation.

Note: This book may produce Americanized Portuguese.

For free sound bytes, visit slanguage.com.

# GREETINGS AND RESPONSES

Are you well?
*Você está bem?*

**Vote Say Stop Bang?**

Good evening
*Boa noite*

**Bow Annoyed**

Good morning
*Bom dia*

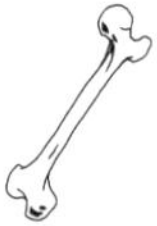

**Bone Dee Ah**

Good-bye
*Adeus*

**Addy Use**

Have a good day
*Tenha um bom dia*

**Tan Yum Bum Dee Ah**

Hello
*Olá*

**Oh Lot**

How are you?
*Como está?*

**Comb Moo Stop?**

How's it going?
*Como tá indo?*

**Comb Moo Tie In Due?**

I don't know
*Eu não sei*

**You Now Say**

I live . . .
*Eu moro . . .*

**You Mode Oh . . .**

May I?
*Posso?*

**Pa Sue?**

Mrs.
*Senhora*

**Seen Yoda**

Nice to meet you
*Prazer em te conhecer*

**Praise Ear Aim 2**

**Quay Ah Say**

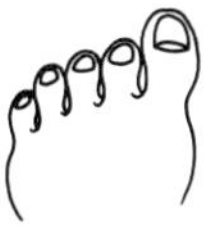

Not too well
*Não muito bem*

**Now Moo We Toe Bang**

Please
*Por favor*

**Pour Fog Vore**

So-so
*Mais ou menos*

**Mice So May Nose**

Thanks
*Obrigado*

**Owe Breeze God Due**

To your health
*À sua saúde*

**Us Sue Ah Saudi**

Welcome
*Bem-vindo*

**Bang Veen Due**

What did you say?
*O que você disse?*

**Okay Vot~~e~~ Say D.C.?**

What's your name?
*Qual o seu nome?*

**Koal~~a~~ Lou Sue No Me?**

What's new?
*O que há de novo?*

**Okay Jaw No Vot~~e~~?**

Where are you from?
*De onde você é?*

**Day Own Due Vote**

**Say Ah?**

Where do you live?
*Onde mora?*

**Own Due Mode Uh?**

You're welcome
*De nada*

**Dee Nod Ah**

# VERBS

To bite
*Morder*

**More Deer**

To copy
*Copiar*

**Cope Pea Odd**

To count
*Contar*

**Cone Todd**

To dance
*Dançar*

**Dan Sod**

To divide
*Dividir*

# Dee Vee Deed

To eat
*Comer*

# Comb Ear

To iron
*Passar a ferro*

# Pass Odd Affair Oh

To jump
*Saltar*

# Saul Todd

To lose weight
*Perder peso*

**Pear Deer Pays Oh**

To make
*Fazer*

**Fuzz Ear**

To paint
*Pintar*

**Pin Todd**

To plant
*Plantar*

**Plan Todd**

To shave
*Barbear*

**Bar Bee Odd**

To sing
*Cantar*

**Can Todd**

To skate
*Patinar*

**Patch a Nod**

To sleep
*Dormir*

**Dorm Ear**

To speak
*Falar*

# Full Odd

To teach
*Ensinar*

# Ain't See Nod

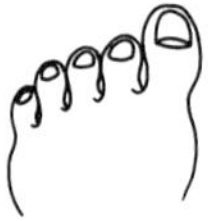

To touch
*Tocar*

# Toe Cod

To wash
*Lavar*

# Love Odd

# ADJECTIVES AND ADVERBS

Almost
*Quase*

**Koala Zee**

Angry
*Zangado*

**Zen God Due**

Bad
*Mau*

**Mouth**

Calm
*Calmo*

**Calm Moo**

Complete
*Completo*

**Comb Play 2**

Crazy
*Louco*

**Low Coo**

Early
*Cedo*

**Say Due**

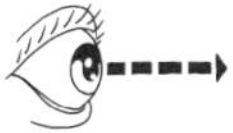

Enough
*Suficiente*

**Sue Fee See Ain't She**

Excited
*Excitado*

**Messy Todd Due**

Full
*Cheio*

**Shay You**

Good
*Bom*

**Bomb**

Handsome
*Belo*

**Bail Lou**

Happy
*Feliz*

**Fell Ease**

Here
*Aqui*

**Ah Key**

Jealous
*Ciumento*

**See You Men 2**

Last
*Último*

**~~P~~ool Tee Moo**

Lazy
*Preguiçoso*

**Preggy Sew Zoo**

A little bit
*Um pouco*

**Boom Poke Coo**

Near
*Perto*

**Pear 2**

New
*Novo*

**No Voo**

Next
*Próximo*

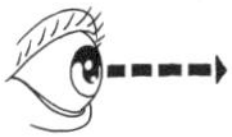

**Praw~~n~~ See Mo~~l~~e**

Old
*Velho*

**Veil Lou**

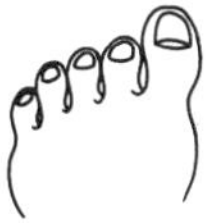

Perfect
*Perfeito*

**Pear Fate Toe**

Pretty
*Bonito*

**Bow Knee 2**

Fast
*Rápido*

**Rap Pea Due**

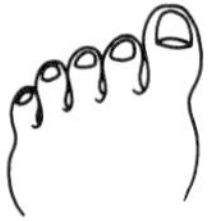

Slow
*Lento*

**Len Toe**

Small
*Pequeno*

**Pick Cane New**

Special
*Especial*

**Ease Best See Al**

Strong
*Forte*

**Forty**

There
*Lá*

**Lot**

Thin
*Fino*

**Fee New**

Thoughtful
*Pensativo*

**Pens Achieve Oh**

Tired
*Cansado*

# Ken Saw Due

Under
*De baixo*

# Due Buy Shoe

Unhappy
*Infeliz*

# In Fell Ease

Useful
*Útil*

# ~~M~~oo Till

Usual
*Comum*

**Comb Boom**

Well
*Bem*

**Bang**

Where
*Onde*

**Own Dee**

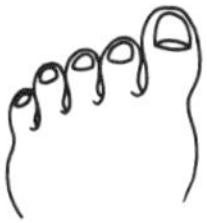

Whole
*Todo*

**Toe Due**

# PRONOUNS, PREPOSITIONS, AND CONJUNCTIONS

And
*E*

**Eek**

Because
*Porque*

**Pour Kay**

But
*Mas*

**Moss**

He
*Ele*

**Eh Lee**

How
*Como*

**Comb Moo**

Me
*Me*

**Me**

Moreover
*Além disso*

**All Lame Dee Sue**

She
*Ela*

**Ella**

Something
*Algo*

**All Goo**

They
*Eles*

**Eh Lease**

With
*Com*

**Comb**

You
*Você*

**Vote Say**

# FRIENDS AND FAMILY

Baby
*Bebê*

**Bay Bee**

Father
*Pai*

**Pie**

A friend
*Um amigo*

**Uma Me Goo**

A grandson
*Um neto*

**Boom Net 2**

Mother
*Mãe*

**My**

A name
*Um nome*

**Boom No Me**

An uncle
*Um tio*

**Boom Tee You**

Widowed
*Viúvo*

**Veal You Voo**

# HOUSEHOLD

Antenna
*Antena*

**Antenna**

Apartment
*Apartamento*

**Apart a Men 2**

Balcony
*Balcão*

**Ball Cow**

Bathroom
*Banheiro*

**Ban Yay Rue**

Bench
*Banco*

**Bang Coo**

Cable
*Cabo*

**Cob Boo**

Oven
*Forno*

**4 New**

Sheet
*Lençol*

**Lynn Saul**

Sofa
*Sofá*

**Sofa**

Stove
*Fogão*

**Foe Gown**

Table
*Mesa*

**Mays Ah**

Trash
*Lixo*

**Lee Shoe**

# TRAVEL

Airport
*Aeroporto*

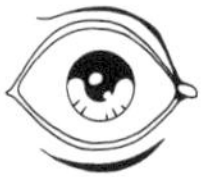

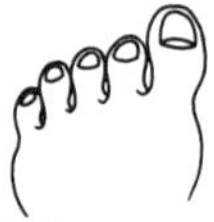

**Eye Row Pour Toe**

American
*Americano*

**Alm Eddy Canoe**

City
*Cidade*

**See Dodgy**

Hotel
*Hotel*

**Oh Tell**

Movie theater
*Cinema*

**See Name Ah**

Museum
*Museu*

**Moo Say Oh**

Nationality
*Nacionalidade*

**Knots Own Olly Dodgy**

North
*Norte*

**Norton**

South
*Sul*

**S~~ch~~ool**

Tour
*Passeio*

**Pass Say You**

Western
*Ocidental*

**Oh See Den Tall**

World
*Mundo*

**Moon Due**

# FOOD AND RESTAURANTS

Cheers!
*Tchin tchin!*

**Chin Chin!**

Do you have . . . ?
*Você tem . . . ?*

**Vote Say Tame . . . ?**

Finished?
*Terminado?*

**Tear Me Nod Oh?**

I'd like . . .
*Gostaria . . .*

**Ghost Odd Dee Ah . . .**

Banana
*Banana*

**Banana**

Beef
*Bife*

**Beefy**

Bread
*Pão*

**Pow**

Breakfast
*Café da manhã*

**Café Dumb ~~A~~mmonia**

Butter
*Manteiga*

**Man Tie Gu~~s~~**

The check
*A conta*

**Ah Cone To~~dd~~**

Coffee
*Café*

**Café**

Delicious
*Delicioso*

**Day Lee See Oh Sue**

Egg
*Ovo*

# Oh Voo

Fish
*Peixe*

# Pay She

Fork
*Garfo*

# Guar~~d~~ Foo

Glass
*Copo*

# Cop Poo

Lemon
*Limão*

**Lee Mow**

Lemonade
*Limonada*

**Lee Moon Nod Ah**

Lunch
*Almoço*

**Almost Sue**

Menu
*Menu*

**May New**

Milk
*Leite*
**Late Tee**

Mushroom
*Cogumelo*
**Coke Goo Mail Lou**

Omelette
*Omelete*
**Oh May Let Tee**

Peach
*Pêssego*
**Pay Say Goo**

Pepper
*Pimenta*

**Pea Men To~~p~~**

Pineapple
*Abacaxi*

**Abba Co~~p~~ She**

Salmon
*Salmão*

**Sal~~t~~ Mow**

Salt
*Sal*

**Sall~~y~~**

Soup
*Sopa*

**Soap Ah**

Sweet
*Doce*

**Doe See**

Tea
*Chá*

**Shop**

Water
*Água*

**Log What**

# BUSINESS AND LABOR

Accountant
*Contador*

**Cone Todd Door**

Accounting
*Contabilidade*

**Cone Top Billy Dodgy**

Bank
*Banco*

**Bank Coo**

Banker
*Banqueiro*

**Bong Kay Roo**

Boss
*Chefe*

**Chef Fee**

Briefcase
*Pasta*

**Pasta**

Doctor
*Médico*

**May Dee Coat**

Farmer
*Fazendeiro*

**Fuzz ’n Day Due**

Firefighter
*Bombeiro*

**Bomb Bay Roo**

Lawyer
*Advogado*

**Odd Vote God Due**

Mail carrier
*Carteiro*

**Car Tay Roo**

Mechanic
*Mecânico*

**May Connie Coat**

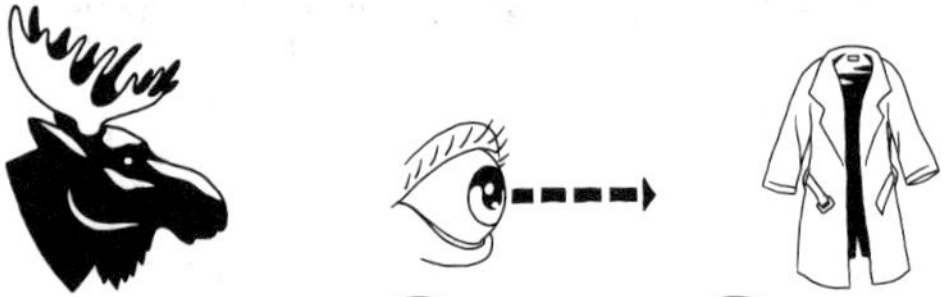

Musician
*Músico*

**Moose See Coa~~t~~**

Painter
*Pintor*

**Pin Tore**

Police officer
*Polícia*

**Poe Lee See You~~ng~~**

Politician
*Político*

**Poe Lee Tee Coa~~t~~**

# TRANSPORTATION

Flight
*Vôo*

# Voo

Gasoline
*Gasolina*

# Gas Oh Lean Ah

Hood
*Capot*

# Cap Poo

Jet
*Jato*

# Jaw 2

Motorcycle
*Moto*

**Moe 2**

Oil
*Óleo*

**Oh Leo**

Port
*Porto*

**Pour 2**

Ship
*Barco*

**Bark Coo**

Sidewalk
*Passeio*

**Pass Say You**

Taxi
*Táxi*

**Tock See**

Train
*Trem*

**Train**

Trunk
*Porta-malas*

**Port Uh Malice**

# EDUCATION

Addition
*Adição*

**Odd Dee Sou~~nd~~**

Backpack
*Mochila*

**Mo~~le~~ Sheila**

Chapter
*Capítulo*

**Cop Pea 2 Lou**

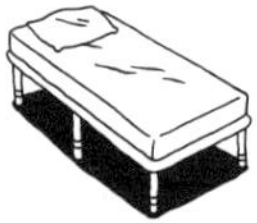

Chemistry
*Química*

**Key Me Co~~t~~**

Course
*Curso*

# Coors Sue

Dictionary
*Dicionário*

# Dee Sewn Audio

Grade
*Nota*

# Note Ah

Idea
*Idéia*

# Eat Day Yac~~ht~~

List
*Lista*

**Least To~~p~~**

Multiplication
*Multiplicação*

**Mole Tee Plea Cuss Sou~~nd~~**

Pen
*Caneta*

**Con Ate To~~p~~**

Physics
*Física*

**Fee Seek Ah**

Pupil
*Aluno*

**Ah Loon New**

A school
*Uma escola*

**Uma's Call Ah**

Sum
*Soma*

**Sew Ma**

Symbol
*Símbolo*

**Seem Bowl Lou**

# SPORTS AND ENTERTAINMENT

Baseball
*Beisebol*

**Baseball**

Bell
*Sino*

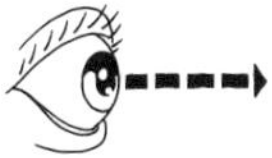

**See New**

Boxing
*Boxe*

**Boxy**

Checkers
*Damas*

**Dam As**

Choir
*Coro*

**Code Due**

Clown
*Palhaço*

**Paul Lasso**

Comedy
*Comédia*

**Comb May Dee Ah**

Cycling
*Ciclismo*

**Seek Liz Mo~~le~~**

Golf
*Golfe*

**Gulf Fee**

Hockey
*Hóquei*

**Okay**

Jogging
*Cooper*

**Coop Ear**

Kite
*Papagaio*

**Papa Guy You**

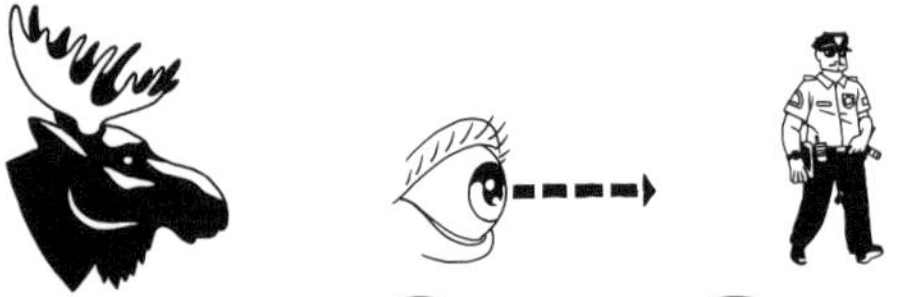

Music
*Música*

**Moose See Cop**

Piano
*Piano*

**Piano**

Singer
*Cantor*

**Can Toad**

Skate
*Patim*

**Pat Team**

Song
*Canção*

**Can Sou~~nd~~**

Swimming
*Natação*

**Not Uh Sou~~nd~~**

Violin
*Violino*

**Vee Oh Lee New**

Whistle
*Assobio*

**Ah Sew Bee You**

# HEALTH AND MEDICINE

Ankle
*Tornozelo*

**Tore Nose Ale Lou**

Arm
*Braço*

**Bra Sew**

Chin
*Queixo*

**Kay Shoe**

To cough
*Tossir*

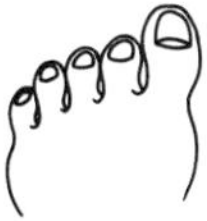

**Toe Seed**

Doctor
*Doutor*

**Doe Tore**

Elbow
*Cotovelo*

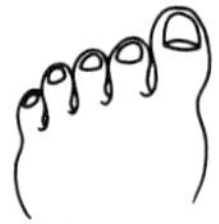

**Coat Toe Veal Lou**

Face
*Cara*

**Cod Ah**

Finger
*Dedo*

**Day Due**

Foot
*Pé*

**Pay**

Hand
*Mão*

**Mou~~nt~~**

Head
*Cabeça*

**Cob Base Ah**

Lip
*Lábio*

**Lobby Oh**

Pill
*Comprimido*

**Comb Pre Me Due**

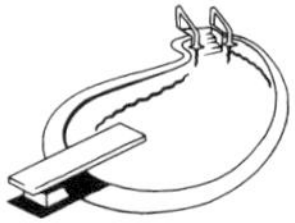

Pulse
*Pulso*

**Pool Sue**

Sick
*Doente*

**Due Went Tee**

Tooth
*Dente*

**Dent Tee**

# MONEY AND SHOPPING

How much does
that cost?
*Quanto isso custa?*

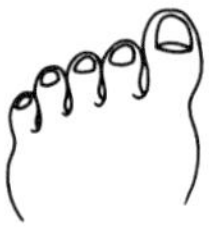

**Kwan Toe Ease Sue Coast Uh**

Is this on sale?
*É este em promoção?*

**Eh Is Chain Promo**

**Say Oh**

Belt
*Cinto*

**Seen 2**

Butcher shop
*Açougue*

**Ah Sew Gee~~k~~**

Button
*Botão*

**Boat Towe~~l~~**

Change
*Troco*

**Tro~~v~~e Coo**

Cotton
*Algodão*

**Al Goo Down**

Dress
*Vestido*

**Vest Tee Due**

Expensive
*Caro*

**Cod Oh**

Handkerchief
*Lenço*

**Len Sue**

Jeans
*Jeans*

**Jeans**

Pair
*Par*

**Pod**

Pocket
*Bolso*

**Bowl Sue**

Price
*Preço*

**Press Sue**

Sale
*Promoção*

**Promo Say Oh**

Scarf
*Cachecol*

**Cash She Call**

Slipper
*Chinelo*

**Shin Ale Lou**

Suit
*Terno*

**Tare New**

Supermarket
*Supermercado*

**Sue Pair Mare Cod Due**

Tailor
*Alfaiate*

**Al Fay Yacht Tee**

T-shirt
*T-shirt*

**Tay Shirt**

Tuxedo
*Smoking*

**Smoking**

# SCIENCE AND NATURE

Birch
*Vidoeiro*

**Vito Eh Roo**

Chemistry
*Química*

**Key Me Cop**

Cloudy
*Nublado*

**New Blah Due**

Daisy
*Margarida*

**Margarita**

Fire
*Fogo*

**Phone Goo**

Lake
*Lago*

**Log Goo**

Ocean
*Oceano*

**Oh See Ann New**

Rain
*Chuva*

**Shoe Vah**

Rocket
*Foguete*

**Foe Get 2**

Sea
*Mar*

**Mod**

Snow
*Neve*

**Navy**

Sun
*Sol*

**Sole**

Sunny
*Ensolarado*

**In Solar Rad Due**

Tulip
*Tulipa*

**2 Leap Ah**

Weather
*Tempo*

**Temp Poe**

Windy
*Ventania*

**Vein 10 Knee Uh**

# NUMBERS AND TIME

One
*Um*

**Boom**

Two
*Dois*

**Doe East**

Three
*Três*

**Tray East**

Four
*Quatro*

**Koala True**

Five
*Cinco*

**Seen Co~~mb~~**

Six
*Seis*

**Say Ease**

Seven
*Sete*

**Set Tee**

Eight
*Oito*

**~~B~~oy 2**

Nine
*Nove*

**No~~d~~ Vee**

Ten
*Dez*

**Des~~k~~**

Eleven
*Onze*

**Own Zee**

Twelve
*Doze*

**Doze Zee**

Hundred
*Cem*

**Same**

Thousand
*Mil*

**Meal**

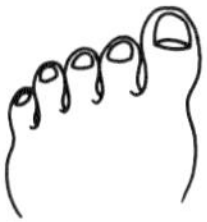

Minute
*Minuto*

**Me New Toe**

Month
*Mês*

**Mace**

New year
*Ano novo*

**Uh New No Voo**

Number
*Número*

**New Maid Oh**

The past
*O passado*

**Ooh Puss Sod Due**

Yesterday
*Ontem*

**Own Tame**